A Picture Book of
Christopher Columbus

David A. Adler

illustrated by John & Alexandra Wallner

Holiday House / New York

Other books in David A. Adler's *Picture Book Biography* series

A Picture Book of George Washington
A Picture Book of Abraham Lincoln
A Picture Book of Martin Luther King, Jr.
A Picture Book of Thomas Jefferson
A Picture Book of Benjamin Franklin
A Picture Book of Helen Keller
A Picture Book of Eleanor Roosevelt

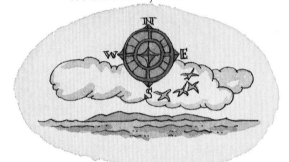

To Samuel Edward Neumark
D.A.A.

Text copyright © 1991 by David A. Adler
Illustrations copyright © 1991 by John C. and Alexandra Wallner
All rights reserved
Printed in the United States of America

Library of Congress Cataloging-in-Publication Data

Adler, David A.
A picture book of Christopher Columbus / by David A. Adler;
illustrated by John C. and Alexandra Wallner.—1st ed.
p. cm.
Summary: A brief account of the life and accomplishments
of Christopher Columbus.
ISBN 0-8234-0857-4
1. Columbus, Christopher—Pictorial works—Juvenile literature
2. Explorers—America—Pictorial works—Juvenile literature.
3. Explorers—Spain—Pictorial works—Juvenile literature.
[1. Columbus, Christopher. 2. Explorers.]
I. Wallner, John C.,
ill. II. Wallner, Alexandra, ill. III. Title.
E111.A27 1991
970.01'5—dc20
[B]   [92]   90-39211   CIP   AC
ISBN 0-8234-0857-4

ISBN 0-8234-0949-X (pbk.)

Christopher Columbus was born in 1451 in Genoa, Italy. His parents were Susanna and Domenico Colombo. Domenico was a master weaver. Susanna was the daughter of a weaver.

Genoa is at the shore of the Ligurian Sea, part of the Mediterranean. When Christopher and others looked out over the water, they saw no end to it.

Christopher was a tall boy with a thin face and freckles. He worked in his father's shop, but he dreamed of going to sea.

When Christopher was young, he took short trips on the sea. When he was older, he became a sailor.

In 1476, when he was twenty-five, Christopher was sailing on one of a group of ships headed for England. French pirates attacked, and the ship on which he was sailing sank. Christopher was injured and thrown into the sea. He grabbed onto some floating wood and made his way to the nearest shore.

Christopher came ashore in Lagos, Portugal. He stayed there until he was well. Then he went to Lisbon, Portugal where his brother Bartholomew lived. Together they ran a shop where they sold maps for sailors and books.

In Lisbon, Christopher married Dona Felipa Moñiz de Perestrello, the daughter of an important family. They had a son, Diego.

People in Lisbon talked of sailing east, around Africa, to the Indies—China, Japan, The East Indies and India— where they could get valuable jewels and spices.

Christopher Columbus and most other people during his time knew the earth was round, but they didn't know how big it was. They had always traveled east to get to the Indies. Columbus thought that he could get there more quickly by sailing in the opposite direction.

Christopher asked King John II of Portugal for three ships to make the voyage. The king refused him.

Christopher's brother Bartholomew went to the kings of France and England. He asked them for the ships Christopher needed to sail west.

They refused, too.

Christopher's wife Felipa died, and he moved to Spain. There he and Beatriz Enriquez de Harana, the daughter of Spanish peasants, had a son, Ferdinand.

Christopher asked King Ferdinand and Queen Isabella of Spain if they could give him money and ships for his voyage west. They were not ready to help either.

Then, in 1492, after years of waiting, the king and queen of Spain finally agreed to help him. They gave him three ships, the *Niña,* the *Pinta,* and the *Santa María,* and about ninety men to sail with him.

On August 3, 1492, the voyage began. Nine days later, the explorers reached the nearby Canary Islands. Then, on September 9, the ships sailed west into the unknown waters of the Atlantic Ocean. The sailors were frightened. At times they wanted to turn back, but Christopher told them, *"Adelante*—Sail on!"

During the first week of October, the men saw birds and other signs of land. And on October 12 they saw land, an island southeast of Florida.

Christopher Columbus and his men rowed ashore. He planted a flag in the sand and claimed the island for Spain. He named it San Salvador.

Christopher Columbus gave the natives of the island red caps and glass bead necklaces. Since he believed his ships had reached the Indies, he named the natives Indians. But they had landed in America, the New World.

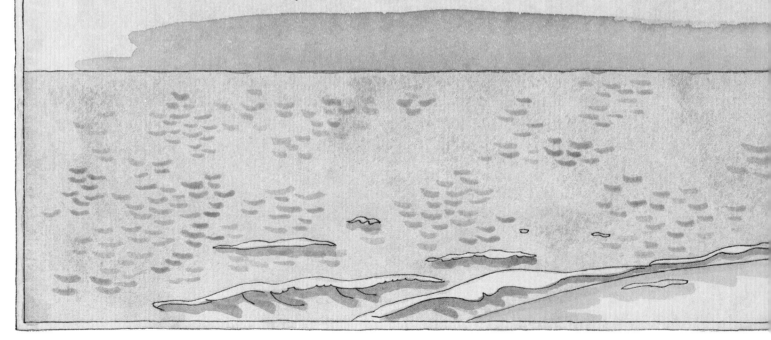

In March 1493 Christopher Columbus sailed back to Spain with gold trinkets, parrots, and a few Indians. He left some sailors in the New World to search for gold.

Christopher was a hero to the people of Spain. King Ferdinand and Queen Isabella named him *Admiral of the Ocean Sea*.

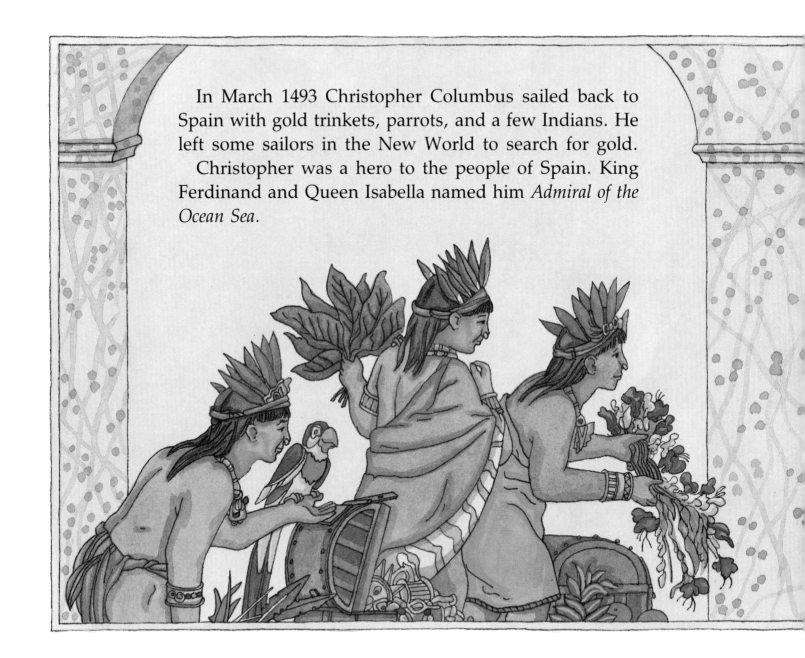

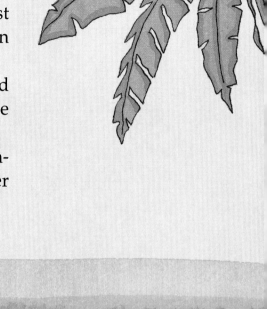

In September 1493, Christopher Columbus sailed west again. This time he led seventeen ships and more than one thousand men.

Christopher found that the men who stayed behind after the first voyage had been cruel to the Indians. The Indians had killed them all.

He found other islands. He set up a colony on Hispaniola, one of the largest islands, and named it Isabela, after the queen.

Columbus sailed to America again in 1498 and 1502. The men who sailed with him had great hopes for gold and other riches. But they found very little gold, and Christopher was no longer a hero.

Even after all four voyages, Christopher Columbus insisted that he had reached the Indies. But he had discovered the land which was later named America.

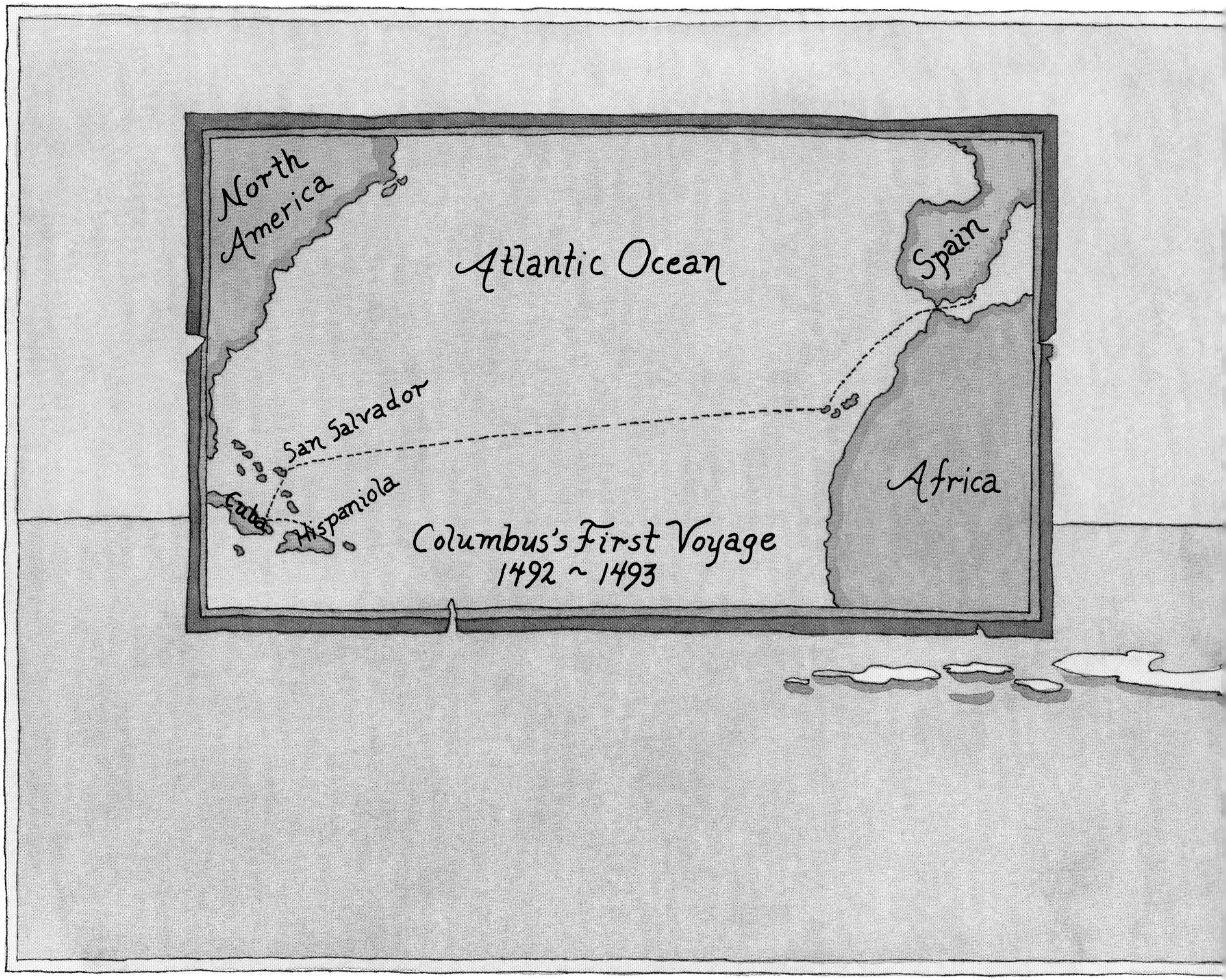

North America

Atlantic Ocean

Spain

San Salvador

Cuba   Hispaniola

Africa

Columbus's First Voyage
1492 ~ 1493

Christopher Columbus died in Valladolid, Spain on May 20, 1506. He had been a great sailor, able to find his way across unknown waters and back home again. He had found the New World.

2

IMPORTANT DATES

1451	Born in Genoa, Italy.
1476	Ship on which he was sailing was attacked. He swam ashore in Lagos, Portugal.
1479	Married Dona Felipa Moñiz de Perestrello.
1480	Son Diego was born.
1486	First asked King Ferdinand and Queen Isabella to finance the voyage. They agreed in January 1492.
1488	Son Ferdinand was born.
1492	Sailed west from Palos, Spain on August 3.
1492	Landed in America on October 12.
1493–1496	The second voyage to America.
1498–1500	The third voyage. Columbus landed on the South American continent.
1502–1504	The fourth voyage.
1506	Christopher Columbus died on May 20 in Valladolid, Spain.